HOW TO BUILD YOUR OWN VPN SERVER

A concise step-by-step VPN guidebook on how to build your own VPN server the easy way

MICHAEL HIROSHI

Table of Contents

CHAPTER ONE

INTRODUCTION

In an age where privacy and security are vital, Virtual Private Networks (VPNs) have emerged as critical tools for protecting our online activity. Commercial VPN services can be pricey and typically have limits. This guidebook seeks to enable you to take control of your online privacy by creating your own VPN server, which will provide you with a cost-effective and customizable solution.

WHY BUILD YOUR OWN VPN SERVER?

Cost savings: Avoid recurrent subscription payments.

Enhanced Privacy: Completely control your data without relying on third-party services.

Customization: Tailor the VPN to meet your requirements and tastes.

Learning Experience: Expand your knowledge and abilities in networking and security.

WHO THIS BOOK IS FOR

This book is intended for novices and budget-conscious customers who want to construct their VPN server. Whether you have little technical experience or are already familiar with basic networking ideas, this guide will take you through the entire procedure step by step.

TOOLS AND RESOURCES NEEDED

A suitable device (such as a Raspberry Pi or an old laptop)

A dependable internet connection.

Basic computing capabilities.

VPN software (such as OpenVPN and WireGuard)

This handbook!

WHAT IS A VPN?

A Virtual Private Network (VPN) is a service that establishes a safe and encrypted connection over an insecure network, such as the Internet. This allows you to maintain your online privacy and secure your data.

BASIC CONCEPTS AND TERMINOLOGY

Encryption is transforming data into a code that prevents unauthorized access.

Tunnel: A secure path via which encrypted data travels.

VPN Server: The server that handles both incoming and outgoing VPN traffic.

VPN Client: A device that connects to a VPN server.

How VPNs Work:

A VPN creates a secure tunnel between your device (the client) and a remote server. All of your internet traffic flows through this tunnel, ensuring that your data is secured and secure. This keeps third parties, including hackers or ISPs, from intercepting your data.

TYPES OF VPNS

Personal VPNs are created by individuals for their usage. They provide complete control over the server and data, making them suitable for users who appreciate privacy and customization.

Commercial VPN services are offered by businesses for a price. They are simple to set up and use, but they may have restrictions and raise privacy problems.

CHAPTER TWO

PLANNING YOUR VPN SETUP

Choosing the Right Hardware

Minimum requirements

CPU: A processor capable of encrypting and decrypting.

RAM: A minimum of 1GB is required for basic use.

Storage: Enough space for the operating system and VPN software.

RECOMMENDED DEVICES

Raspberry Pi: A cost-effective, compact, and efficient VPN server.

Old Laptop: Convert an old laptop with decent hardware into a more powerful VPN server.

Dedicated Mini-PCs are small form factor PCs that are meant to run continuously.

Selecting the Software

Choosing the correct software for your VPN server is critical to delivering a seamless and safe experience. There are various popular VPN software alternatives available, each with unique benefits and capabilities. In this part, we'll look at two popular VPN software options: OpenVPN and WireGuard.

OPENVPN

OpenVPN is a versatile and frequently used VPN program that has existed since 2001. It is renowned for its durability, adaptability, and strong security features.

Pros:

OpenVPN is highly configurable, allowing you to personalize your VPN setup to your exact needs.

Strong Security: It supports several encryption methods and protocols, guaranteeing that your data is protected.

Cross-Platform Support: OpenVPN is compatible with Windows, macOS, Linux, iOS, and Android.

Community Support: Because OpenVPN is a well-established program, it has a big user base and rich documentation, making it easy to locate assistance and resources.

Cons:

Complex Setup: OpenVPN's comprehensive capabilities might make the setup procedure difficult, particularly for beginners.

While OpenVPN is secure, it may be slower than newer VPN protocols due to its more complex encryption methods.

Use Cases: Perfect for users seeking a personalized and secure VPN solution.

Suitable for applications where compatibility with a variety of devices is required.

WIREGUARD

WireGuard is a relatively new VPN protocol that has gained popularity because to its simplicity, speed, and robust security. It was created to be easier to configure and use than traditional VPN protocols such as OpenVPN.

Pros:

Simplicity: WireGuard's design is straightforward, making it easy to install and configure.

High Performance: WireGuard is noted for its speed and efficiency, which outperforms earlier protocols.

Strong Security: It employs advanced cryptographic techniques to ensure robust security.

Cross-Platform Support: WireGuard is available for

Windows, macOS, Linux, iOS, and Android.

Small Codebase: WireGuard's minimal codebase is easier to audit and maintain, lowering the chance of security breaches.

Cons:

WireGuard is a newer protocol, with fewer features and a smaller user base than OpenVPN.

Limited Customization: Although WireGuard is extremely efficient, it provides fewer customization choices than OpenVPN.

Ideal for users who value performance and ease of setup.

Suitable for situations when simplicity and speed are critical.

CHOOSING BETWEEN OPENVPN AND WIREGUARD

When choosing between OpenVPN and WireGuard, consider the following factors:

Ease of Setup: If you are a beginner or prefer a simple setup process, WireGuard may be a better option.

WireGuard outperforms other products in terms of speed and efficiency.

Customization and capabilities: If you require a VPN that is extremely adjustable and has a wide range of capabilities, OpenVPN is the better option.

Community and Support: OpenVPN's lengthy history and big user base imply better resources and community support.

Both OpenVPN and WireGuard are excellent solutions for setting up your own VPN server. Your decision should be based on your requirements, technical comfort, and desired features. In the following chapters, we will provide extensive instructions for configuring both OpenVPN and WireGuard, allowing you to select the one that best meets your needs.

CHAPTER THREE

SETTING UP THE HARDWARE

PREPARING YOUR DEVICE

Setting up your device entails installing an operating system (OS), which will act as the foundation for your VPN server. The technique varies slightly based on the hardware being used. In this section, we will go over how to install the Raspberry Pi OS and Ubuntu.

INSTALLING AN OPERATING SYSTEM

Raspberry Pi OS

Raspberry Pi OS (formerly known as Raspbian) is the official operating system for the Raspberry Pi. It is lightweight and optimized for the Raspberry Pi hardware.

STEPS TO INSTALL RASPBERRY PI OS:

Download the Raspberry Pi imager:

Raspberry Pi Downloads is the official website for the Raspberry Pi.

Download the Raspberry Pi Imager for your operating system (Windows, Mac OS, or Linux).

Prepare the microSD card:

Use a card reader to connect your microSD card to your computer.

Launch the Raspberry Pi Imager.

Open the Raspberry Pi Imager app.

Click "CHOOSE OS" and choose "Raspberry Pi OS (32-bit)".

Click "CHOOSE SD CARD" and choose your microSD card.

Click "WRITE" to begin the installation procedure.

Insert a microSD card into your Raspberry Pi.

After the writing procedure is completed, remove the microSD card from your computer.

Insert the microSD card into the Raspberry Pi.

Power on your Raspberry Pi:

Connect the Raspberry Pi to a power source.

Connect a monitor, keyboard, and mouse to the Raspberry Pi.

Initial Setup:

To finish the initial setup, follow the on-screen instructions, which include selecting a language and time zone, as well as creating an account.

Update your system by opening a terminal and running the following commands:

sudo apt update

sudo apt upgrade –y

UBUNTU

Ubuntu is a popular Linux distribution that can be used on a variety of hardware, including old laptops and desktops. It is user-friendly and well-supported.

STEPS TO INSTALL UBUNTU:

Download the Ubuntu ISO:

Visit the official Ubuntu website: Ubuntu Downloads.

Download the latest version of the Ubuntu ISO file.

Create a Bootable USB Drive:

Use a tool like Rufus (for Windows) or Etcher (for macOS and Linux) to create a bootable USB drive with the Ubuntu ISO.

Insert your USB drive into your computer and launch the chosen tool.

Select the Ubuntu ISO file and your USB drive, then click "Start" to create the bootable USB drive.

Boot from the USB Drive:

Insert the bootable USB drive into your target computer.

Power on the computer and enter the BIOS/UEFI settings (usually by pressing a key like F2, F12, DEL, or ESC during startup).

Change the boot order to prioritize the USB drive.

Save the settings and exit the BIOS/UEFI.

Install Ubuntu:

The computer will boot from the USB drive and load the Ubuntu installer.

Follow the on-screen instructions to install Ubuntu. Select "Install Ubuntu" and proceed with the setup.

Choose your language, keyboard layout, and installation type (for beginners, it's recommended to use the "Erase disk and install Ubuntu" option).

Create a user account and set up your system preferences.

Click "Install Now" and wait for the installation to complete.

Initial Setup:

After installation, remove the USB drive and reboot the computer.

Complete the initial setup, including system updates. Open a terminal and run the following commands:

sudo apt update

sudo apt upgrade –y

SETTING UP THE HARDWARE

Connecting with the Network

Your VPN server must be connected to your network to function effectively. There are two primary methods for connecting your device to the network: wired (Ethernet) and wireless (Wi-Fi).

WIRED VS. WIRELESS CONNECTIONS

The advantages of using a wired connection (Ethernet) include increased stability and reliability.

Generally faster than Wi-Fi.

There is less interference from other devices.

Disadvantages: Requires an Ethernet cable and router port.

Placement is less flexible (your device must be near the router).

Wireless Connection (Wi-Fi) Advantages:

Greater freedom in device positioning.

There's no need for physical cords.

Disadvantages: Can be less stable and slower than Ethernet.

It is susceptible to interference from other devices and networks.

Steps to connect:

To make a wired connection, connect one end of an Ethernet cable to your device and the other to an available router port.

During the initial configuration of your operating system (Raspberry Pi OS or Ubuntu), choose a Wi-Fi network and input the password.

BASIC DEVICE CONFIGURATION

Once your device is connected to the network, you'll need to complete some basic configuration tasks, such as initial setup and upgrades.

INITIAL SETUP AND UPDATES

Raspberry Pi OS:

To power on your Raspberry Pi, connect it to a power source.

Connect a monitor, keyboard, and mouse to the Raspberry Pi.

Insert the microSD card with the Raspberry Pi OS installed.

Follow the onscreen instructions:

Choose your nation, language, and time zone.

Set up a user account with a username and password.

If you're utilizing a wireless connection, connect to your Wi-Fi network.

Update Your System:

Open a terminal by clicking on the terminal icon in the taskbar or pressing `Ctrl + Alt + T.`

Type the following commands to update your system:

sudo apt update

sudo apt upgrade –y

Ubuntu:

Connect your device (laptop, desktop, etc.) to a power source.

Connect a monitor, keyboard, and mouse as needed.

Insert the bootable USB disk containing Ubuntu installed.

Follow the onscreen instructions:

When the installer loads, select "Install Ubuntu".

Select your language, keyboard layout, and installation type.

Set up a user account with a username and password.

If you're utilizing a wireless connection, connect to your Wi-Fi network.

Update Your System:

Once the installation is complete
and you've booted into Ubuntu,
open a terminal by pressing `Ctrl`
`+ Alt + T`.

Type the following commands to
update your system:

sudo apt update

sudo apt upgrade -y

CHAPTER FOUR

INSTALLING THE VPN SOFTWARE

INSTALLING OPENVPN

Step-by-Step Installation Guide

OpenVPN is a popular and robust VPN option. Follow these instructions to install OpenVPN on your device:

Update Your System:

Open a terminal and run the following commands to ensure your system is up to date:

sudo apt update

sudo apt upgrade –y

Install OpenVPN:

Install OpenVPN by running the following command:

sudo apt install openvpn –y

Install Easy-RSA:

Easy-RSA is a tool for managing certificate authority (CA), private keys, and certificates. Install it using the following command:

sudo apt install easy-rsa –y

Set Up the CA Directory:

Create a directory for Easy-RSA and navigate to it:

make-cadir ~/openvpn-ca

cd ~/openvpn-ca

Edit the `vars` File:

Open the `vars` file in a text editor and customize the following variables to match your information (e.g., country, province, city):

nano vars

Example variables to edit:

set_var   EASYRSA_REQ_COUNTRY "US"

set_var   EASYRSA_REQ_PROVINCE "California"

set_var   EASYRSA_REQ_CITY "San Francisco"

set_var   EASYRSA_REQ_ORG "MyVPN"

set_var   EASYRSA_REQ_EMAIL "email@example.com"

set_var   EASYRSA_REQ_OU "MyVPNUnit"

Build the Certificate Authority (CA):

Initialize the environment and build the CA:

source vars

./clean-all

./build-ca

Generate the Server Certificate and Key:

Create the server certificate and key:

```
./build-key-server
server
```

Generate Diffie-Hellman Parameters:

Create the Diffie-Hellman parameters for key exchange:

```
./build-dh
```

Generate Client Certificates and Keys:

Create a client certificate and key *(repeat this step for each client):*

```
./build-key client1
```

CONFIGURE OPENVPN:

Copy the sample server configuration file and edit it to match your setup:

```
sudo                    cp
/usr/share/doc/openvpn/
examples/sample-config-
files/server.conf.gz
/etc/openvpn/
```

```
sudo                gunzip
/etc/openvpn/server.con
f.gz
```

```
sudo                  nano
/etc/openvpn/server.con
f
```

Edit the configuration file as needed (e.g., setting paths to keys and certificates).

START THE OPENVPN SERVER:

Start the OpenVPN server service:

```
sudo systemctl start openvpn@server
```

Enable OpenVPN to Start on Boot:

Enable the OpenVPN service to start on boot:

```
sudo systemctl enable openvpn@server
```

INSTALLING WIREGUARD

Step-by-step installation guide:

WireGuard is a modern, high-performance VPN system. Follow these steps to set up WireGuard on your device:

Update Your System:

Open a terminal and run the following commands to ensure your system is up to date:

```
sudo apt update
sudo apt upgrade -y
```

INSTALL WIREGUARD:

Install WireGuard by running the following command:

```
sudo apt install wireguard -y
```

Generate Keys:

Create a directory for your keys and navigate to it:

```
mkdir -p ~/wireguard-keys
```

```
cd ~/wireguard-keys
```

Generate private and public keys for the server:

```
umask 077
```

```
wg      genkey      |     tee
privatekey  |  wg  pubkey
> publickey
```

Configure WireGuard:

Create and edit the WireGuard configuration file:

```
sudo                  nano
/etc/wireguard/wg0.conf
```

Example   configuration   file (`wg0.conf`):

```
[Interface]
PrivateKey                    =
<YourPrivateKey>
```

Address = 10.0.0.1/24

ListenPort = 51820

[Peer]

PublicKey =
<ClientPublicKey>

AllowedIPs = 10.0.0.2/32

START THE WIREGUARD INTERFACE:

Bring up the WireGuard interface:

sudo wg-quick up wg0

Enable WireGuard to Start on Boot:

Enable the WireGuard service to start on boot:

```
sudo systemctl enable wg-quick@wg0
```

ALTERNATIVE VPN SOFTWARE OPTIONS

A Brief Overview of Other Software

While OpenVPN and WireGuard are popular alternatives, there are numerous additional VPN software options available, each with its own set of capabilities and use cases.

SoftEther VPN:

Pros: Supports multiple protocols, including OpenVPN, L2TP/IPsec, and MS-SSTP.

High performance and versatility.

Cons: Setup is more complex than other VPN applications.

Pritunl: Pros: User-friendly web interface.

Supports OpenVPN and WireGuard.

Cons: The web interface requires additional setup.

StrongSwan offers robust IPsec implementation.

Strong security features.

Cons: Difficult to configure, especially for novices.

Pros of ZeroTier include its ease of setup and management.

Works as both a VPN and an SD-WAN solution.

Cons: Limited control over the underlying network architecture.

Each of these alternative VPN software alternatives provides distinct advantages and may be better suited to specific requirements or preferences. For most users, beginning with OpenVPN or WireGuard will give a great basis for developing a dependable and secure VPN server.

CHAPTER FIVE

CONFIGURING THE VPN SERVER

Basic Configuration

Configuring your VPN server entails creating the necessary keys and certificates, adding and managing user accounts, and adjusting parameters to improve performance and security.

GENERATING KEYS AND CERTIFICATES

FOR OPENVPN:

Set Up the CA Directory:

Navigate to the Easy-RSA directory:

cd ~/openvpn-ca

Build the Certificate Authority (CA):

Initialize the environment and build the CA

source vars

./clean-all

./build-ca

Generate the Server Certificate and Key:

Create the server certificate and key:

./build-key-server server

Generate Diffie-Hellman Parameters:

Create the Diffie-Hellman parameters for key exchange:

./build-dh

Generate Client Certificates and Keys:

Create a client certificate and key (repeat this step for each client):

./build-key client1

FOR WIREGUARD:

Generate Server Keys:

Create a directory for your keys and navigate to it:

mkdir -p ~/wireguard-keys

cd ~/wireguard-keys

Generate private and public keys for the server:

umask 077

wg genkey | tee privatekey | wg pubkey > publickey

Generate Client Keys:

For each client, generate a pair of private and public keys:

wg genkey | tee client1_privatekey | wg pubkey > client1_publickey

SETTING UP USER ACCOUNTS

Managing user accounts involves generating and distributing configuration files for each user.

FOR OPENVPN:

Generate Client Certificates and Keys:

Repeat the steps in the "Generating Keys and Certificates" section for each new client.

Example for a second client:

cd ~/openvpn-ca

source vars

./build-key client2

Create Client Configuration Files:

Copy the sample client configuration file and customize it for each user:

sudo   cp /usr/share/doc/openvpn/examples

/sample-config-files/client.conf

/etc/openvpn/client1.conf

sudo nano
/etc/openvpn/client1.conf

Ensure the paths to the client's keys and certificates are correctly set.

Distribute Configuration Files:

Provide each user with their customized configuration file, client certificate, and key.

FOR WIREGUARD:

Create Client Configuration Files:

For each client, create and edit a configuration file:

sudo   nano /etc/wireguard/client1.conf

Example client configuration file:

[Interface]

PrivateKey = <Client1PrivateKey>

Address = 10.0.0.2/24

[Peer]

PublicKey = <ServerPublicKey>

Endpoint = <YourServerIP>:51820

AllowedIPs = 0.0.0.0/0

PersistentKeepalive = 21

Distribute Configuration Files:

Provide each user with their customized configuration file and their private key.

ADVANCED CONFIGURATION

Optimizing your VPN server entails changing settings for improved performance and security.

Configuring Settings for Performance and Security

FOR OPENVPN:

Optimize Server Configuration:

Edit the server configuration file to improve performance:

sudo nano /etc/openvpn/server.conf

Example optimizations:

push "redirect-gateway def1 bypass-dhcp"

push "dhcp-option DNS 8.8.8.8"

push "dhcp-option DNS 8.8.4.4"

keepalive 10 120

comp-lzo

user nobody

group nogroup

persist-key

persist-tun

Enhance Security:

Implement additional security measures in the server configuration file:

tls-auth ta.key 0

cipher AES-256-CBC

auth SHA256

Implement Two-Factor Authentication (Optional):

Set up two-factor authentication using Google Authenticator or another TOTP app.

FOR WIREGUARD:

Optimize Server Configuration:

Edit the server configuration file to improve performance and security:

sudo nano /etc/wireguard/wg0.conf

Example optimizations:

```
[Interface]

PrivateKey = <YourPrivateKey>

Address = 10.0.0.1/24

ListenPort = 51820

SaveConfig = true

[Peer]

PublicKey = <Client1PublicKey>

AllowedIPs = 10.0.0.2/32
```

Enhance Security:

Ensure strong cryptographic settings are in place and regularly update the server and clients.

Network Settings:

Configure your firewall to allow WireGuard traffic:

sudo ufw allow 51820/udp

Enable Logging and Monitoring:

Set up logging and monitoring to track VPN usage and detect potential issues.

ENABLING LOGGING AND MONITORING FOR OPENVPN

Enable logging in openvpn:

OpenVPN can be configured to log various events. By default, OpenVPN logs are written to the system log. You can customize the log file and verbosity level.

Edit the OpenVPN Server Configuration:

Open the OpenVPN server configuration file:

sudo   nano
/etc/openvpn/server.conf

Add or modify the following lines
to enable logging:

 # Log file location

log-append /var/log/openvpn.log

 # Log verbosity level (0-11)

verb 3

 # Status file

status /var/log/openvpn-status.log

Save and close the file.

Restart OpenVPN Service:

Apply the changes by restarting the OpenVPN service:

sudo systemctl restart openvpn@server

Monitor OpenVPN Logs:

To view the logs, you can use the tail command:

tail -f /var/log/openvpn.log

The status log provides information about current connections:

cat /var/log/openvpn-status.log

Enabling logging and monitoring for wireguard

Enable Logging in WireGuard:

WireGuard itself doesn't have extensive logging capabilities built in, but you can use the system's logging tools to monitor WireGuard activity.

Edit the WireGuard Configuration File:

Open the WireGuard configuration file:

sudo   nano /etc/wireguard/wg0.conf

Add the following lines to enable basic logging:

```
[Interface]

PrivateKey = <YourPrivateKey>

Address = 10.0.0.1/24

ListenPort = 51820

SaveConfig = true


[Peer]

PublicKey = <ClientPublicKey>

AllowedIPs = 10.0.0.2/32
```

Save and close the file.

Set Up System Logging for WireGuard:

Configure the system's logging service (systemd) to capture WireGuard logs.

Create a Systemd Service Override:

Create a directory for the service override:

sudo mkdir -p /etc/systemd/system/wg-quick@wg0.service.d

Create an override file:

```
sudo nano /etc/systemd/system/wg-quick@wg0.service.d/override.conf
```

Add the following content to the file:

[Service]

ExecStartPre=/bin/sh -c 'echo $(date) Starting WireGuard >> /var/log/wireguard.log'

ExecStartPost=/bin/sh -c 'echo $(date) WireGuard started >> /var/log/wireguard.log'

ExecStopPost=/bin/sh   -c   'echo $(date)   WireGuard   stopped   >> /var/log/wireguard.log'

Save and close the file.

Reload Systemd Daemon:

Apply the changes by reloading the systemd daemon:

sudo systemctl daemon-reload

sudo   systemctl   restart   wg-quick@wg0

Monitor WireGuard Logs:

To view the WireGuard logs, use the tail command:

tail -f /var/log/wireguard.log

Additional Monitoring Tools

For more comprehensive monitoring, you can use tools like Prometheus and Grafana, or VPN-specific monitoring tools like vnStat and Netdata.

Installing and Configuring vnStat:

Install vnStat:

sudo apt install vnstat –y

Configure vnStat:

sudo nano /etc/vnstat.conf

Ensure the configuration matches your network interface (e.g., eth0).

Start and Enable vnStat:

sudo systemctl start vnstat

sudo systemctl enable vnstat

View Network Usage:

vnstat

Installing and Configuring Netdata:

Install Netdata:

bash <(curl -Ss https://my-netdata.io/kickstart.sh)

Access Netdata:

Open a web browser and go to

http://<your-server-ip>:19999 to

access the Netdata dashboard.

CHAPTER SIX

NETWORK CONFIGURATION

PORT FORWARDING

Port forwarding is necessary for routing VPN traffic to your server. This step includes setting your router to accept VPN traffic via a certain port.

CONFIGURING YOUR ROUTER

Step-by-Step Guide to Configure Port Forwarding:

Access Your Router's Web Interface:

Open a web browser and enter your router's IP address in the address bar. Common IP addresses include `192.168.0.1`, `192.168.1.1,` or `192.168.1.254`.

Log in using your router's username and password (check the router manual or sticker for default credentials).

Find the Port Forwarding Section:

Navigate to the port forwarding section, often found under settings like "Advanced", "NAT", "Firewall", or "Virtual Server".

Create a Port Forwarding Rule:

Add a new rule for your VPN server. Fill in the details as follows:

Name/Description: Enter a name for the rule (e.g., "VPN Server").

External Port: Enter the port number your VPN server listens on (default is `1194` for OpenVPN and `51820` for WireGuard).

Internal Port: Same as the external port.

Protocol: Select `UDP` (or `TCP/UDP` for OpenVPN if needed).

Internal IP Address: Enter the local IP address of your VPN server (e.g., `192.168.1.100`).

Save the Settings:

Save or apply the new port forwarding rule.

Reboot Your Router (if necessary):

Some routers may require a reboot to apply the changes.

DYNAMIC DNS

Dynamic DNS (DDNS) allows you to access your VPN server using a consistent domain name, even if your public IP address changes.

SETTING UP DYNAMIC DNS FOR EASIER ACCESS

Step-by-Step Guide to Set Up Dynamic DNS:

Choose a Dynamic DNS Provider:

Select a DDNS provider (e.g., No-IP, DynDNS, DuckDNS).

Create an Account:

Sign up for an account on the DDNS provider's website.

Create a Hostname:

Follow the provider's instructions to create a hostname (e.g., `myvpn.ddns.net`).

Configure Your Router to Use DDNS:

Log in to your router's web interface.

Navigate to the DDNS settings, often found under "Dynamic DNS", "DDNS", or similar.

Enter the following details:

Service Provider: Select your DDNS provider.

Hostname: Enter the hostname you created.

Username/Email: Enter your DDNS account username or email.

Password/Key: Enter your DDNS account password or API key.

Save the Settings:

Save or apply the DDNS settings.

Firewall Settings

Configuring your firewall is crucial to securing your VPN server and ensuring only authorized traffic is allowed.

ENSURING YOUR VPN IS SECURE

Step-by-Step Guide to Configure Firewall Settings:

FOR OPENVPN:

OpenVPN Firewall Rules:

Open a terminal and create firewall rules to allow VPN traffic:

sudo ufw allow 1194/udp

sudo ufw allow OpenSSH

Enable UFW (Uncomplicated Firewall):

Enable UFW and check the status:

sudo ufw enable

sudo ufw status

Configure ip forwarding:

Enable IP forwarding to allow traffic to pass through the VPN server:

sudo nano /etc/sysctl.conf

Uncomment or add the following line:

net.ipv4.ip_forward=1

Apply the changes:

sudo sysctl -p

Add NAT Rules:

Create NAT rules to route traffic from the VPN to your local network:

sudo nano /etc/ufw/before.rules

Add the following lines before the *filter line:

*nat

:POSTROUTING ACCEPT [0:0]

-A POSTROUTING -s 10.8.0.0/8 -o eth0 -j MASQUERADE

COMMIT

FOR WIREGUARD:

WireGuard Firewall Rules:

Open a terminal and create firewall rules to allow VPN traffic:

```
sudo ufw allow 51820/udp
```

```
sudo ufw allow OpenSSH
```

Enable UFW (Uncomplicated Firewall):

Enable UFW and check the status:

```
sudo ufw enable
```

```
sudo ufw status
```

Configure IP Forwarding:

Enable IP forwarding to allow traffic to pass through the VPN server:

```
sudo                    nano
/etc/sysctl.conf
```

Uncomment or add the following line:

```
net.ipv4.ip_forward=1
```

Apply the changes:

```
sudo sysctl -p
```

Add NAT Rules:

Create NAT rules to route traffic from the VPN to your local network:

```
sudo                    nano
/etc/ufw/before.rules
```

Add the following lines before the `*filter` line:

```
*nat

:POSTROUTING          ACCEPT
[0:0]

-A      POSTROUTING      -s
10.0.0.0/24  -o  eth0  -j
MASQUERADE

COMMIT
```

CHAPTER SEVEN

CONNECTING TO YOUR VPN

Client Software Installation

To connect to your VPN server, first install VPN client software on your devices. The following are the recommended VPN clients for various devices.:

Recommended VPN Clients for Various Devices

For OpenVPN:

Windows:

Download and install the OpenVPN client from the OpenVPN website.

Mac:

Download and install Tunnelblick from the Tunnelblick website.

iOS:

Install the OpenVPN Connect app from the App Store.

Android:

Install the OpenVPN Connect app from the Google Play Store.

For WireGuard:

Windows:

Download and install the WireGuard client from the WireGuard website.

Mac:

Download and install the WireGuard client from the WireGuard website.

iOS:

Install the WireGuard app from the App Store.

Android:

Install the WireGuard app from the Google Play Store.

CONFIGURATION FILES

Configuration files are required for connecting to your VPN server. These files contain the settings and credentials required for establishing a secure connection.

Exporting and Importing Configuration Files

For OpenVPN:

Exporting Configuration Files:

On your VPN server, navigate to the OpenVPN directory where the client configuration files are stored.

Typically, the client configuration file is named `client.ovpn`.

Copy the client certificate (`client.crt`), key (`client.key`), and CA certificate (`ca.crt`) to the same directory as the `client.ovpn` file.

Importing Configuration Files on Windows:

Open the OpenVPN client and click on "Import".

Select the `client.ovpn` file to import the configuration.

Importing Configuration Files on Mac (Tunnelblick):

Open Tunnelblick and click on "I have configuration files".

Drag and drop the `client.ovpn` file into the Tunnelblick window.

Importing Configuration Files on iOS and Android:

Transfer the `client.ovpn` file to your device.

Open the OpenVPN Connect app and tap on "File" to import the configuration file.

For WireGuard:

Exporting Configuration Files:

On your VPN server, create a client configuration file for WireGuard.

Example client configuration file (`client.conf`):

[Interface]

PrivateKey = <ClientPrivateKey>

Address = 10.0.0.2/24

DNS = 8.8.8.8

[Peer]

PublicKey = <ServerPublicKey>

Endpoint = <YourServerIP>:51820

AllowedIPs = 0.0.0.0/0

PersistentKeepalive = 25

Importing Configuration Files on Windows and Mac:

Open the WireGuard client.

Click on "Import tunnel(s) from file" and select the `client.conf` file.

Importing Configuration Files on iOS and Android:

Transfer the `client.conf` file to your device.

Open the WireGuard app and tap on the "+" button to import the configuration file.

CONNECTING AND TROUBLESHOOTING

After installing the client software and importing the configuration files, you can connect to your VPN.

TESTING THE CONNECTION

OpenVPN:

Open the OpenVPN client and select the imported configuration.

Click "Connect" to initiate the connection.

Check the log for any connection messages and ensure it connects successfully.

WireGuard:

Open the WireGuard client and select the imported configuration.

Click "Activate" to initiate the connection.

Check the status to ensure it connects successfully.

COMMON ISSUES AND FIXES

Issue: Connection Timed Out

Cause: The server may not be reachable or the port may be blocked.

Fix:

Ensure the server is online and accessible.

Verify port forwarding rules on your router.

Check firewall settings on both the server and the client.

Issue: Authentication Failed

Cause: Incorrect credentials or certificates.

Fix:

Verify the client configuration file contains the correct certificates and keys.

Ensure the server and client configurations match.

Issue: No Internet Access After Connecting

Cause: Incorrect routing or DNS settings.

Fix:

Ensure the server configuration pushes the correct routes to the client.

Verify the DNS settings in the client configuration file.

Issue: Slow Connection Speeds

Cause: Network congestion or server performance issues.

Fix:

Test the network speed independently to isolate the issue.

Optimize server settings and consider upgrading hardware if necessary.

CHAPTER EIGHT

MAINTAINING YOUR VPN SERVER

Regular Updates

Keeping your software and operating system up-to-date is essential to protect your VPN server from vulnerabilities and to ensure it runs smoothly.

Keeping Your Software and OS Up-to-Date

Step-by-Step Guide for Regular Updates:

Update the Operating System:

Open a terminal on your VPN server.

Run the following commands to update your system's package list and upgrade installed packages:

```
sudo apt update
```

```
sudo apt upgrade -y
```

Update OpenVPN:

Ensure you have the latest version of OpenVPN installed:

```
sudo apt install openvpn -y
```

Update WireGuard:

Ensure you have the latest version of WireGuard installed:

```
sudo       apt       install
wireguard -y
```

Schedule Regular Updates:

Consider setting up automatic updates to ensure your system is always up-to-date. Edit the `apt` configuration to enable automatic updates:

```
sudo                 nano
/etc/apt/apt.conf.d/50u
nattended-upgrades
```

Ensure the following lines are present:

```
Unattended-
Upgrade::Allowed-
Origins {

"${distro_id}:${distro_
codename}-security";

};
```

Save the file and configure the unattended-upgrades package:

```
sudo dpkg-reconfigure -
-priority=low
unattended-upgrades
```

MONITORING AND LOGGING

Monitoring your VPN server helps you keep an eye on usage, performance, and potential issues. Proper logging can assist in troubleshooting and maintaining security.

KEEPING AN EYE ON USAGE AND PERFORMANCE

Step-by-Step Guide for Monitoring and Logging:

Set Up Logging for OpenVPN:

Open the OpenVPN server configuration file:

sudo nano /etc/openvpn/server.conf

Add or modify the following lines to enable logging:

log-append /var/log/openvpn.log

verb 3

status /var/log/openvpn-status.log

Save and restart the OpenVPN service:

```
sudo systemctl restart openvpn@server
```

Set Up Logging for WireGuard:

Create a logging configuration for WireGuard:

sudo mkdir -p /etc/systemd/system/wg-quick@wg0.service.d

sudo nano /etc/systemd/system/wg-quick@wg0.service.d/override.conf

Add the following lines

[Service]

ExecStartPre=/bin/sh -c 'echo $(date) Starting WireGuard >> /var/log/wireguard.log'

ExecStartPost=/bin/sh -c 'echo $(date) WireGuard started >> /var/log/wireguard.log'

ExecStopPost=/bin/sh -c 'echo $(date) WireGuard stopped >> /var/log/wireguard.log'

Save and reload the systemd daemon:

sudo systemctl daemon-reload

sudo systemctl restart wg-quick@wg0

Monitor Logs:

View OpenVPN logs:

```
tail                    -f
/var/log/openvpn.log
```

View WireGuard logs:

```
tail                    -f
/var/log/wireguard.log
```

Install and Configure Monitoring Tools:

Netdata: A comprehensive monitoring tool that provides real-time performance metrics.

```
bash <(curl -Ss
https://my-
netdata.io/kickstart.sh
)
```

Access the Netdata dashboard via
```
http://<your-server-
ip>:19999.
```

BACKUPS AND RECOVERY

Regular backups and a recovery plan are essential to ensure that you can restore your VPN server in case of hardware failure, data corruption, or other issues.

Ensuring You Can Restore Your Server

Step-by-Step Guide for Backups and Recovery:

Backup Configuration Files:

Create a directory for backups:

```
mkdir -p ~/vpn-backups
```

Copy OpenVPN configuration and keys:

```
cp -r /etc/openvpn ~/vpn-backups/
```

```
cp -r ~/openvpn-ca ~/vpn-backups/
```

Copy WireGuard configuration and keys:

```
cp -r /etc/wireguard ~/vpn-backups/
```

Automate Backups:

Set up a cron job to automate the backup process. Open the crontab editor:

```
crontab -e
```

Add a cron job to run the backup script daily:

```
0    2    *    *    *
/usr/bin/rsync        -a
/etc/openvpn
/etc/wireguard
/home/username/vpn-
backups/
```

Store Backups Offsite:

Consider storing backups in a secure offsite location, such as a cloud storage service (e.g., Google Drive, Dropbox) or an external hard drive.

Create a Recovery Plan:

Document the steps needed to restore your VPN server from backups.

Test the recovery process periodically to ensure you can quickly restore the server when needed.

Example Recovery Steps:

Reinstall the Operating System:

Follow the installation steps for Raspberry Pi OS or Ubuntu as outlined in Chapter 3.

Restore Configuration Files:

Copy the backed-up configuration files to their original locations:

```
sudo cp -r ~/vpn-backups/openvpn /etc/

sudo cp -r ~/vpn-backups/wireguard /etc/
```

Restart VPN Services:

Restart OpenVPN:

```
sudo systemctl restart
openvpn@server
```

Restart WireGuard:

```
sudo systemctl restart
wg-quick@wg0
```

CHAPTER NINE

ADVANCED SECURITY FEATURES

Adding sophisticated security features protects your VPN server from illegal access and potential threats. Here, we'll go over how to set up two-factor authentication and intrusion detection systems.

Two Factor Authentication (2FA)

Adding two-factor authentication (2FA) improves security by requiring a second type of verification in addition to the normal password.

Step-by-Step Guide to Set Up Two-Factor Authentication:

Install Google Authenticator:

Install the Google Authenticator PAM module on your VPN server:

```
sudo apt install libpam-google-authenticator
```

Configure OpenVPN for 2FA:

Open the OpenVPN configuration file:

```
sudo nano /etc/openvpn/server.conf
```

Add the following line to enable PAM authentication:

```
plugin
/usr/lib/openvpn/openvp
n-plugin-auth-pam.so
login
```

Configure PAM to Use Google Authenticator:

Edit the PAM configuration file for OpenVPN:

```
sudo                nano
/etc/pam.d/openvpn
```

Add the following line:

```
auth                    required
pam_google_authenticato
r.so
```

Set Up Google Authenticator for Each User:

Run the following command for each user to set up Google Authenticator:

```
google-authenticator
```

Follow the prompts to configure 2FA and save the generated QR code and secret key.

INTRUSION DETECTION SYSTEMS (IDS)

An intrusion detection system (IDS) helps monitor your network for suspicious activity and potential threats.

Step-by-Step Guide to Set Up IDS with Snort:

Install Snort:

Install Snort on your VPN server:

```
sudo apt install snort
```

Configure Snort:

Open the Snort configuration file:

```
sudo                    nano
/etc/snort/snort.conf
```

Modify the configuration to match your network settings (e.g., HOME_NET).

Start Snort:

Start the Snort service to begin monitoring:

```
sudo    systemctl    start
snort
```

Monitor Snort Alerts:

View Snort alerts by checking the log file:

```
cat /var/log/snort/alert
```

OPTIMIZING PERFORMANCE

Optimizing the performance of your VPN server ensures better speed and reliability for users. Here, we'll cover how to tweak settings for better speed and reliability for both OpenVPN and WireGuard.

Tweaking Settings for Better Speed and Reliability

Step-by-Step Guide to Optimize OpenVPN Performance:

Optimize Encryption Settings:

Open the OpenVPN configuration file:

```
sudo          nano
/etc/openvpn/server.con
f
```

Modify the cipher settings for better performance:

```
cipher AES-128-GCM

ncp-ciphers AES-128-GCM
```

Enable Compression:

Add the following line to enable compression:

```
compress lz4
```

Adjust MTU Settings:

Add the following lines to adjust the MTU settings:

```
tun-mtu 1500
```

```
mssfix 1400
```

Increase the Number of Concurrent Connections:

Add the following line to increase the maximum number of clients:

```
max-clients 100
```

Restart OpenVPN:

Apply the changes by restarting the OpenVPN service:

```
sudo systemctl restart openvpn@server
```

Step-by-Step Guide to Optimize WireGuard Performance:

Use Efficient Ciphers:

WireGuard uses highly efficient ciphers by default, so no additional configuration is typically needed.

Adjust MTU Settings:

Open the WireGuard configuration file:

```
sudo                nano
/etc/wireguard/wg0.conf
```

Add the following line to adjust the MTU settings:

```
MTU = 1420
```

Enable and Configure BBR TCP Congestion Control:

Enable BBR by adding the following lines to your `/etc/sysctl.conf` file:

net.core.default_qdisc=fq

net.ipv4.tcp_congestion_control=bbr

Apply the changes:

```
sudo sysctl -p
```

Restart WireGuard:

Apply the changes by restarting the WireGuard service:

```
sudo systemctl restart wg-quick@wg0
```

PRIVACY CONSIDERATIONS

Ensuring that your VPN protects your privacy is critical to preserving secrecy and security.

Ensure Your VPN Protects Your Privacy.

Step-by-Step Guide to Enhance Privacy:

Disable Logging (if necessary):

To enhance privacy, you can disable logging in your VPN configuration. Be aware that this may make troubleshooting more difficult.

For openvpn:

sudo   nano /etc/openvpn/server.conf

Comment out or remove the log
directives:

#log-append /var/log/openvpn.log

#status /var/log/openvpn-status.log

For WireGuard:

sudo nano
/etc/wireguard/wg0.conf

Comment out or remove any
logging configurations.

Use Strong Encryption:

Ensure your VPN is configured to use strong encryption methods to protect your data.

For OpenVPN:

cipher AES-256-CBC

auth SHA256

For WireGuard, strong encryption is used by default.

To prevent vulnerabilities, update your VPN software and operating system regularly (see Chapter 8 for instructions).

Monitor for Leaks:

Use online tools to detect DNS, IP, and WebRTC leaks while connected to your VPN. Make sure your VPN isn't disclosing your true IP address.

Educate users:

Inform your users about best privacy practices, such as not transmitting personal information via unprotected connections.

TROUBLESHOOTING AND FAQS

CONNECTIVITY ISSUES

VPN Connection Timed Out

Cause: The VPN server may not be reachable or the port may be blocked.

Solution:

Verify that the VPN server is online and accessible.

Ensure the correct port forwarding rules are set up on your router (refer to Chapter 6).

Check firewall settings on both the server and the client to ensure the VPN port is allowed.

Authentication Failed

Cause: Incorrect credentials or certificates.

Solution:

Verify that the client configuration file contains the correct certificates and keys.

Ensure the server and client configurations match.

No Internet Access After Connecting

Cause: Incorrect routing or DNS settings.

Solution:

Ensure the server configuration pushes the correct routes to the client.

Verify the DNS settings in the client configuration file.

For OpenVPN, ensure the following lines are in the server configuration:

push "redirect-gateway def1 bypass-dhcp"

push "dhcp-option DNS 8.8.8.8"

push "dhcp-option DNS 8.8.4.4"

PERFORMANCE PROBLEMS

Slow Connection Speeds

Cause: Network congestion, server performance issues, or suboptimal configuration.

Solution:

Test the network speed independently to isolate the issue.

Optimize server settings (refer to Chapter 9).

Consider upgrading server hardware if necessary.

Ensure the client and server are using efficient encryption ciphers.

Frequent Disconnections

Cause: Unstable network connection or server configuration issues.

Solution:

Check the stability of your internet connection.

Ensure keep-alive settings are configured properly:

keepalive 10 120

For WireGuard:

PersistentKeepalive = 25

Frequently Asked Questions.

What is a VPN?

A VPN (Virtual Private Network) establishes a secure, encrypted connection between your device and a remote server, allowing you to browse the internet in privacy and security.

Why should I use my own VPN server?

Using your own VPN server provides you complete control over your data, promotes privacy, and removes the recurring membership fees that come with commercial VPN services.

What VPN software should I use: OpenVPN or WireGuard?

Both have advantages. OpenVPN is extremely flexible and widely supported, but WireGuard provides simplicity, excellent performance, and robust security. Choose according to your personal requirements and technical comfort level.

How do I update my VPN server software?

Regularly update your system by running:

sudo apt update

sudo apt upgrade -y

How can I monitor my VPN server's performance?

Use monitoring tools like Netdata or system logs to keep an eye on usage and performance (refer to Chapter 8).

Can I use my VPN server on multiple devices?

Yes, you can configure multiple clients by generating separate client configuration files and keys for each device.

GETTING HELP

Community and Online Resources

The OpenVPN community forum is an excellent resource for asking problems and finding solutions. OpenVPN Community Forum

Wireguard Mailing List:

The WireGuard mailing list is a helpful resource for asking questions and addressing issues: Wireguard Mailing List

Reddit Communities:

Various subreddits are dedicated to VPNs and networking, such as:

r/VPN

r/selfhosted

r/HomeNetworking

Stack Exchange Network:

Ask questions and find answers on forums like Stack Overflow and Server Fault:

Stack Overflow

Server Fault

Official Documentation:

Refer to the official documentation for OpenVPN and WireGuard for detailed guides and troubleshooting tips:

OpenVPN Documentation

WireGuard Documentation

By referring to these resources, you can find help and solutions to any issues you may encounter. Maintaining a secure and well-performing VPN server involves regular updates, monitoring, and troubleshooting, but with the right tools and knowledge, you can ensure a reliable and private internet experience.

APPENDICES

Glossary of Terms

VPN (Virtual Private Network): A service that creates a secure, encrypted connection over a less secure network, such as the internet.

OpenVPN: A popular open-source VPN software that uses SSL/TLS for key exchange and supports multiple protocols.

WireGuard: A modern, high-performance VPN protocol that

aims to be faster and simpler than traditional VPN protocols.

IP Address: A unique address assigned to each device connected to a network, allowing it to communicate with other devices.

DNS (Domain Name System): A system that translates human-friendly domain names (e.g., www.example.com) into IP addresses.

PAM (Pluggable Authentication Modules): A mechanism for integrating multiple low-level authentication schemes into a high-level API.

Encryption: The process of converting data into a code to prevent unauthorized access.

Port Forwarding: A network technique that redirects a communication request from one address and port number combination to another.

Firewall: A security system that controls incoming and outgoing network traffic based on predetermined security rules.

2FA (Two-Factor Authentication): An additional layer of security requiring two forms of verification before granting access.

IDS (Intrusion Detection System): A device or software application that monitors a network or systems for malicious activity or policy violations.

MTU (Maximum Transmission Unit): The size of the largest protocol data unit that can be communicated in a single network layer transaction.

ADDITIONAL RESOURCES

Books

"Mastering OpenVPN" by Eric F Crist and Jan Just Keijser: A comprehensive guide to setting up and managing an OpenVPN server.

"Linux Networking Cookbook" by Carla Schroder: Covers various aspects of Linux networking, including VPN setup.

"WireGuard: Next Generation Secure Networking" by Jason A. Donenfeld: An in-depth look at WireGuard and its features.

Websites

OpenVPN Official Site: https://openvpn.net

WireGuard Official Site: https://www.wireguard.com

No-IP (Dynamic DNS): https://www.noip.com

DuckDNS (Dynamic DNS): https://www.duckdns.org

Forums

OpenVPN Community Forum: https://forums.openvpn.net/

WireGuard Mailing List: https://lists.zx2c4.com/mailman/listinfo/wireguard

Reddit r/VPN: https://www.reddit.com/r/VPN/

Reddit r/selfhosted: https://www.reddit.com/r/selfhosted/

Reddit r/HomeNetworking: https://www.reddit.com/r/HomeNetworking/

Sample Configurations

Example Configuration Files for Reference

OpenVPN Server Configuration (/etc/openvpn/`server.con`
`f`):

port 1194

proto udp

dev tun

ca ca.crt

cert server.crt

key server.key

dh dh.pem

server 10.8.0.0 255.255.255.0

ifconfig-pool-persist ipp.txt

```
push      "redirect-gateway      def1
bypass-dhcp"

push "dhcp-option DNS 8.8.8.8"

push "dhcp-option DNS 8.8.4.4"

keepalive 10 120

tls-auth ta.key 0

cipher AES-256-CBC

auth SHA256

comp-lzo

user nobody

group nogroup

persist-key
```

persist-tun

status /var/log/openvpn-status.log

log-append /var/log/openvpn.log

verb 3

OpenVPN Client Configuration (client.ovpn):

client

dev tun

proto udp

remote your_server_ip 1194

resolv-retry infinite

nobind

```
user nobody

group nogroup

persist-key

persist-tun

ca ca.crt

cert client.crt

key client.key

remote-cert-tls server

tls-auth ta.key 1

cipher AES-256-CBC

auth SHA256

comp-lzo
```

verb 3

WireGuard Server Configuration (`/etc/wireguard/wg0.conf`):

[Interface]

PrivateKey = <ServerPrivateKey>

Address = 10.0.0.1/24

ListenPort = 51820

SaveConfig = true

[Peer]

PublicKey = <Client1PublicKey>

AllowedIPs = 10.0.0.2/32

WireGuard Client Configuration (client.conf):

[Interface]

PrivateKey = <ClientPrivateKey>

Address = 10.0.0.2/24

DNS = 8.8.8.8

[Peer]

PublicKey = <ServerPublicKey>

Endpoint = your_server_ip:51820

AllowedIPs = 0.0.0.0/0

PersistentKeepalive = 25

THE END